Which One Is Not Like the Others?

A BOOK ABOUT DIFFERENCES

BY NICK REBMAN

Published by The Child's World®
1980 Lookout Drive • Mankato, MN 56003-1705
800-599-READ • www.childsworld.com

Acknowledgments
The Child's World®: Mary Swensen, Publishing Director
Red Line Editorial: Editorial direction and production
The Design Lab: Design

Photographs ©: Shutterstock Images, cover (top left), cover
(bottom right), 4, 5 (background), 6–7 (background), 8–9,
11 (red flowers), 12; Jiri Hera/Shutterstock Images, cover (top
right); Sergiy Kuzmin/Shutterstock Images, cover (bottom left);
Sean Donohue Photo/Shutterstock Images, 5 (foreground);
Jiang Hongyan/Shutterstock Images, 6–7 (sneakers); Kucher
Serhii/Shutterstock Images, 7 (black shoes); Nolte Lourens/
Shutterstock Images, 7 (boy); Margouillat Photo/Shutterstock
Images, 9 (fruit); Sergey Novikov/Shutterstock Images, 10–11;
Mandy Godbehear/Shutterstock Images, 13

ISBN 9781503807686
LCCN 2015958111

Printed in the United States of America
Mankato, MN
June, 2016
PA02306

About the Author

Nick Rebman likes to write, draw, and travel. He lives in Minnesota.

Some things are similar. Some things are different. Can you figure out which one is not like the others?

Nellie is at the park. She has seeds in her hand. She likes to feed the birds.

Which bird is not like the others?

Matt loves shoes.
He has many
pairs. They are all
different colors.

Which shoes
are not like
the others?

7

Carly is feeling hungry. She goes to the kitchen. She sees four bowls on the table.

Carson likes being outside. He sits in a field. He sees many flowers.

Which flower is not like the others?

11

Molly likes playing sports. She sees lots of balls on the ground.

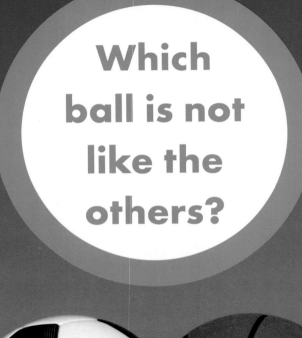

Which
ball is not
like the
others?

ANSWER KEY

The white bird
is not like the others.

The black shoes are
not like the others.

The fruit bowl is not like the others.

The red flower is
not like the others.

The football is not
like the others.

GLOSSARY

different (DIFF-er-ent) Things that are different are not the same. The red flower was different from the others.

similar (SIM-uh-ler) Things that are similar have parts in common. Many of Matt's shoes were similar to each other.

TO LEARN MORE

IN THE LIBRARY

Handford, Martin. *Where's Waldo? Deluxe Edition*. Somerville, MA: Candlewick Press, 2012.

Pistoia, Sara. *Shapes*. Mankato, MN: Child's World, 2014.

Weber, Bob. *Go Fun! Spot Six Differences*. Kansas City, MO: Andrew McMeel Publishing, 2015.

ON THE WEB

Visit our Web site for links about differences: childsworld.com/links

Note to Parents, Teachers, and Librarians: We routinely verify our Web links to make sure they are safe and active sites. So encourage your readers to check them out!

INDEX